Acknowledgments

This book is dedicated to our very own Eclectus parrot, Gizmo.

Table of contents

Prologue

Buying a parrot is a decision that should not be taken lightly: after all, some parrots can live up to 80 years! Are you ready to take on such a responsibility? Will you still want a parrot 10 years from now? Do you have the time to spend at least 3-4 hours with your parrot every day? Are you ready to clean up pieces of fresh fruit and vegetables from your floor and walls every day? To clean you parrot's cage (this is certainly not a glamorous job)? To prepare fresh fruit and vegetables every day? Can you handle the ear-piercing scream that some parrots can let out at 6 am in the morning? Or the screams that last for 10 minutes? Are you ready to get rid of all the non-stick pots and pans in your house? To give up perfume and candles? Are you OK with being bitten occasionally (and sometimes this can really hurt!)?

And finally, are you capable of handling more love than you thought was ever possible for these little bundles of joy? If you answered yes to all of these, then read on- this book may just be the one for you!

Gizmo-Introduction to our very own Eclectus

Gizmo is a four-year-old Eclectus parrot who entered our lives when he was just three months olds. He is the joy of our life and brings a smile to our faces every day. I could dedicate a whole book just to the thousand facets of his personality. When we were first looking into buying a parrot, it was not an easy choice. Amongst all the different breeds out there and each one being so different and interesting, we had a difficult time deciding what species of parrot to choose. Before approaching a breeder for the first time, we did a lot of research to make sure that the parrot we would choose would be suited to our lifestyle and our habits. We knew that we wanted a relatively independent bird who could entertain himself when we were out of the house. We also wanted a parrot with good talking abilities and a high level of intelligence. Another important deciding factor was the noise level- as we lived in an apartment, we did not want to choose a noisy species such as sun conures who would keep our neighbours up all night. Having had a vague idea of what we were looking for and list of suitable breeds, we decided to go for it and met with a reputable breeder. When we met Gizmo, it was love at first sight – his adorable green cheeks and curious nature were all we needed to make our decision! He is now the centre of our lives and the source of much entertainment both for us and our families. This book is dedicated partly to him, but mostly it is here for all the people who are thinking of buying a parrot and are considering getting an Eclectus. This book will not provide you with a detailed anatomy of an Eclectus nor their breeding habits in the wild. This information you can find on any

Eclectus website. Instead, and more importantly, this is a book written from one Eclectus owner to another and based entirely off our experiences. We hope that you will find all of the information that you need in this book to be able to make an informed decision as to whether an Eclectus is the right fit for your household. Finally, we hope to give you an insight into what it is like to own these little green, adorable monsters.

The Eclectus parrot: a brief introduction

Let's first start off by describing your average Eclectus: Eclectus parrots are medium-sized, stocky parrots with a short tail and large beak. One of the most interesting characteristics of Eclectus parrots are that they are sexually dimorphic (this means that males and females look entirely different to each other. When these parrots were first discovered in the wild, the males and females were even thought to be different species! Male Eclectuses like Gizmo have a bright green plumage with red feathers on their sides and under their wings and bright blue feathers on the edge of their wings. Their beaks range from yellow to orange, to almost red. Most Eclectus tails will have a yellow band at the bottom.

Female Eclectuses have a bright red plumage with purple feathers on the chest and under the wings. Female beaks are black in colour. Younger Eclectus parrots are born with a brown beak which will fade to yellow for males and darken to black for females. There are eight to ten different subspecies of Eclectus, the most popular in captivity being the Solomon Island and Grand eclectus.

Eclectus parrots are native to the tropical rainforests of New Guinea, the Solomon Islands, parts of Australia and the Moluccan islands, amongst others. On average Eclectuses are between 40 and 50 centimeters when measured from tail to the beak and generally weigh between 360 grams and 510 grams depending on the subspecies.
Eclectuses generally have a lifespan of around 30-60 years depending on their lifestyle and the conditions in which they are kept in captivity.

What are Eclectuses really like? An insight into the Eclectus mind.

When you meet an Eclectus for the first time, your first impression may be that the species is lethargic, boring and does not have much of a personality at all. However, this is completely wrong- Electuses can be quite shy around new people or new situations and therefore will 'freeze' when they are stressed. Therefore, an Eclectus may act completely different around a stranger than around their family. We experienced this first hand with Gizmo- whilst he is a talkative, playful and a naughty bundle of joy when he is with us, as soon as we have visitors in the house (particularly if he has never met them before), he will sit still in his corner of the play stand and shyly observe the 'intruders' from a distance. Although he is very gentle with us, if a curious stranger tries to stroke him, he will most likely leave with a bite mark on his finger.

Generally, Eclectuses have a relatively calm and shy temperament- they love to simply sit on a branch for hours and watch you go about your daily business. Unlike many other parrot breeds, they are not particularly demanding in terms of attention and are perfectly capable of entertaining themselves. They are pensive birds who do not adapt well to a busy and chaotic household- if you have three kids, two dogs and love loud music then this species may not be the best choice. Eclectuses absolutely love their routines. They do not do well with chaos and changes and much prefer to know exactly what time you get back home each day, when exactly they are fed and what time they go to bed. If you do not provide your Eclectus with a stable and routine environment then he will let you know it by screaming, biting or generally being more aggressive.

Eclectuses are considered one of the most intelligent parrot breeds (often compared to African greys) and are capable of solving children's puzzles and having a large vocabulary of words. Some Eclectuses' are even able to say certain words in context. Gizmo has a large vocabulary of words and will certainly use some words in context such as:

-Bye Bye (when we leave the house)
-Night night (when he is tired and it is time for bed)
-Naughty (you guessed it- when he knows he is doing something wrong)
-Peek-a-boo (when we cover his eyes with our hands)

Additionally, some of the other more interesting sentences he knows include "I'm a chicken" (this is a good party trick), "talk to me" and songs such as "If you're happy and you know it". Despite their great ability to talk, Eclectuses are generally considered to be a quieter species and therefore often considered amongst the better species for apartments. However, whilst Eclectuses do not make noise as often as some other breeds, when they do decide to scream then it can be quite deafening. So whilst Eclectuses may be better suited for apartments than sun conures for example, you are never safe from a loud shriek or two. With Gizmo we have found that the above is completely true- whilst he loves to talk and sing and will do so frequently, he very rarely screams or makes loud noises. Occasionally he will get overexcited and let out a few loud shrieks but these do not occur on a daily basis and do not seem to have disturbed our neighbours (so far).

People often ask at what age Eclectuses start to speak. This is completely dependent on the individual- some start as early as 3 months of age whilst others say their first words when they turn 3 years of age. Some may not speak at all, but this is generally quite rare. Gizmo learnt his first words as soon as we got him at the age of three months ("I love you" and "step up" were some of his first words). We spent a lot of time talking to him every day and teaching him phrases (using a high-pitched voice is often a good idea as parrots tend to prefer mimicking a high pitch). You can also stimulate your parrot's talking abilities by turning on the radio or TV when you are out of the house, actively teaching it words and phrases, and even singing songs. The more 'interesting' you make a word sound, such as exaggerating the intonation or saying it with a funny voice, the more likely your parrot will learn to say it. Of course, don't forget that certain words are easier for parrots to pronounce than others. Words that have the letter C, K , G or T are often easier to pronounce than words that have the letters 'S, Z or F.

Intelligence often comes with being more sensitive-this means that you should make sure to have enough time to spend with your parrot everyday or it will start to feel neglected and stressed. We have noticed the more time we spend with Gizmo, the more social and loving he is. On the days where unfortunately he has to stay longer in his cage he will often be angry or annoyed. With Eclectuses, intelligence and sensitivity often go hand in hand. Unfortunately this means that they are one of the species (alongside African greys and cockatoos) prone to destructive behaviours such as feather plucking. Excluding any diseases, a good diet and calm environment should normally help reduce this behaviour (although this is not always the case). Further details on feather plucking and ways to stop it can be found in later chapters.

Whilst Eclectuses are generally friendly and gentle, around a year and a half to three years (depending partly on the sub species), Eclectuses start to sexually mature and this means that they can be particularly aggressive or aloof. Try not to take this too personally, your Eclectus is simply growing up and going through hormonal changes. Once this phase has passed, you will find that your Eclectus will go back to its usual self. When comparing female and male Eclectuses, owners often find that the female is slightly more moody, independent and aggressive than the male. This is no surprise as the female is the dominant gender in the wild. However, this observation is based entirely on the opinion of a few of our friends who own Eclectus females and should not in any way discourage you from getting a female Eclectus. You should simply be aware that in general, female Eclectuses can throw more frequent tantrums than males, but can be just as cuddly and friendly as males.

A lot of people have asked us if Electuses are cuddly parrots. The answer, as always, is that it depends what you consider 'cuddly'. Generally speaking, Eclectuses are not the cuddliest parrots out there – if you are looking for a parrot that will lie on its back on your hand and close its eyes whilst you stroke its cheeks, then you should probably get a cockatoo or a green cheeked conure. Eclectuses have their own version of cuddliness: they will love to sit on your shoulder or your hand for hours on end and have their beaks kissed. However, they often do not like to be touched on their heads or the rest of their body in general. Gizmo is relatively cuddly for an Eclectus and loves to have his head stroked, but this is generally the exception rather than the rule. If I had to compare an Eclectus to a person I would say they have the personality of an aristocrat; poised, proud, elegant and enjoying your companionship but do not try and cuddle them too much or they will get offended.

Despite all of the above, please do not forget that every Eclectus is an individual- some males may be particularly aggressive whilst others may never speak a single word. Some could be loud and unsuitable for apartments and others could not like to be touched at all. However, if you choose a young Eclectus parrot then more often than not you can to an extent shape the personality and behaviours of the bird based on your environment and how you raise it.

Reading your Eclectuses' body language:

Parrots cannot always tell us exactly how they feel (wouldn't that be great!), but they can certainly show us. As a parrot owner, you need to be able to read your parrot's body language at all times as this will make both your and their life much easier and prevent any misunderstandings. Below are some tips for reading your parrot's body language:

<u>Tail wagging</u>

Parrots will sometimes wag their tails very quickly from side to side. This usually happens when they are about to do something they like (for example when they are about to take a shower or see you coming home after work). Sometimes, tail wagging can also happen right before your parrot is about to change its activity and do something different (for example start playing with a new toy). Generally, tail wagging indicates a happy parrot. Gizmo in particular, loves to wag his tail when he hears the shower being turned on as this is one of his all-time favourite activities.

Beak Grinding

Your parrot will most likely grind its beak when it is tired and falling asleep. Beak grinding helps to keep the beak sharpened and is a sign of a happy, relaxed and content bird. There is nothing better than having a parrot sit on your shoulder, fluff up and grind its beak in the evening: the definition of happiness!

Regurgitation

If your parrot regurgitates on you or an object, it usually means that it is showing you/the object affection and most likely considers you/the object its mate. Whilst this may seem cute, this behaviour should not be encouraged as it can lead to behavioural problems later on such as aggression or frustration. In order to prevent sexual frustration in your parrot you should avoid the following activities where your parrot could consider you as a potential mate:

-stroking your parrot on its back or under its wings
-feeding your parrot warm, mashed food (this replicates regurgitation for them)
-some owners have noticed increased sexual aggression or frustration if they allow their parrots to sit for long times on their shoulder or at 'eye-level'. We dispute this fact as we have not noticed any change in Gizmo's behaviour when he sits on our shoulders for several hours (which he loves to do).

Biting

Biting can come in different degrees and can mean different things. Obviously, a sharp painful bite means that your parrot is either frightened, angry or trying to dominate you. However, what many owners consider a 'bite' is often just a parrot who lightly grabs hold of your finger to either explore your hands or balance itself when you pick it up. This should not normally hurt as the parrot is simply exerting some pressure from its beak rather than lunging or biting. Therefore, this behaviour should not be punished in any way. If your parrot is regularly biting you then you need to carefully examine the reasons behind this: is you parrot sexually frustrated? Is it bored/lonely? Does it receive an adequate diet? Is it scared of you? Trying to figure out the reasons why you parrot is biting you can then help you to find the best ways to deal with this behaviour. Do not forget that younger parrots that are growing up and hormonally maturing are exploring their boundaries and finding out what their limits are so some biting is to be expected. If this happens, try not to react too much as this will encourage your parrot. Either put it back on its playstand or cage, say a firm 'NO' or shake your hand slightly as this will unbalance your parrot and hopefully discourage it from further bites.

Pinning Eyes

If you notice that our parrot is looking at you or an object and its iris shrinks and enlarges repeatedly then it means one of two things depending on the situation:

1- your parrot is angry or frightened (this usually goes along with tightly pressed wings and elongation of the body)

2-your parrot is excited and curious about something (if your parrot's body is relaxed and it is simply pinning its eyes with a tilted head then it is most likely just very curious about something or analysing something intently).

Introducing a second parrot

Introducing a second (or more) parrots is a very personal choice. Often people worry that their parrot is lonely. Others think that introducing a friend will help combat destructive behaviour such as feather plucking, screaming or aggression. On a positive side, the birds will form a bond, entertain and preen each other. However, you need to be aware that a second parrot also means double the mess, cleaning, expenses and noise. There is also the chance that the two parrots will not get along, which means that you need to spend more time interacting with both separately. Sometimes your parrot could react badly to the 'intruder' who is now stealing your time and affection. Always make sure not to neglect your first parrot and give it extra attention in order to prevent jealousy. If you think that your birds is lonely or bored, it is sometimes a better idea to try and introduce new toys, put the radio on or just spend more time with your bird rather than buying a new parrot straightaway.

Many parrots, especially if they have been the only bird in the house for a long time, may see their human as part of their flock and not necessarily want or need another bird. This is often the case for Eclectus parrots that do very well as the only pet in the household. Gizmo is alone, yet treated like a King- not once has he showed any signs of boredom or loneliness as he considers us his 'flock'. However, many species of smaller parrots such as budgies and conures do well when they have several parrots of their species to keep them company.

If you do decide to buy a second parrot, always make sure that the species of bird will fit in well with your current lifestyle. If you have a shy, quiet Eclectus parrot who likes his calm environment, you may not want to introduce a loud, active and boisterous cockatoo. Size is also very important- there is more danger in introducing two birds of very different sizes as the stronger bird could very easily injury or even kill the smaller bird.

Quarantine: Always make sure to quarantine a new bird when bringing it home. Normally the quarantine period should be between 30 and 60 days as several illnesses only make an appearance after 30 days.

Quarantine set-up: During this period, your bird should be kept in a separate room from your existing flock. This is important to protect your flock from any airborne illnesses. As you are trying to prevent any contagious diseases from spreading, make sure to pay careful attention to sanitation:

-wash your hands each time after handling the new bird
-Use separate food bowls and toys

Introducing your birds

Parrots will generally prefer others of their own species and size. Usually smaller parrots such as budgies will be easier to integrate into a flock than larger parrots such as Eclectuses.

Ingredients for a successful introduction:

-Have separate cages for your parrots in the same room. This way they can see each other whilst having their own space.

-Make sure to spend time separately with each parrot outside of its cage

-Your first parrot should be given special attention in order to avoid jealousy: feed it first and take it out of his cage first for instance.

The next Steps

Once your parrots have been kept in the same room for some time, the next step is to introduce them on a neutral space: a good idea is to provide a new playstand where they can get to know each other and play together whilst still having enough space to get away in case of any fights. Birds that are out together should be constantly monitored - in case of any signs of aggression or jealousy, quickly separate the birds.

Tricks to help your parrots bond

-One way to make your parrots positively associate with each other is by using snacks: when they are both out of their cage give them several treats. This will help them to see the experience of being outside together as a positive one. You can even try and teach them some tricks together whilst they are out as this can help them bond by doing activities together. Keep a close eye to make sure that no jealousy occurs.

-Sometimes, letting your birds see you interact with the new bird can help them accept the new flock member. However, sometimes this can have the opposite effect: the older birds can become jealous. You need to keep an eye out and judge the situation.

 Do not forget that your first bird has become used to a certain routine, whereas your new bird has no expectations. This means that the new bird should adapt to the older birds' routine rather than vice versa.

In general, having separate cages for your parrots is always best as they will have their own private space and there is less danger of injury. However, if you are intent on housing two birds together, please follow the steps listed above and make sure that the two birds are interacting positively when out on the perch together. Once you are sure that the two birds get along relatively well, then you can start to leave them in an open cage together for a couple of hours at first with strict supervision. If all goes well, you can then increase the time they are together in the cage until you feel comfortable to leave them alone. However, always make sure that there are perches on different levels, two separate food and water bowls for each so that no rivalry over food occurs. In general, two younger parrots will be more likely to accept living together in a cage from the very start than an older parrot that is used to being alone.

A lot of people wonder whether their parrot will become less friendly if it bonds with the new bird. This depends on each parrot, but generally speaking if you make sure to spend enough time with each separately this should normally not occur.

Taking your parrot outside

Training your parrot to wear a harness is a great way to expand your Parrot's world by taking it outside in all safety but without the constraints of a cage. By taking your parrot outside in a harness, it will be able to get fresh air and sunlight (both essential factors for a parrot's health), meet new people and better adapt to changes in its environment. A parrot that is used to being in different situations will be easier to leave at your friend's house when you are on holiday or to bring to the vet. If you enjoy talking long walks, then harness training your parrot will allow you to spend more time together outside of the house.

It is important to slowly desensitise your parrot to being taken outside step by step. You can start by taking your parrot out in a small travel cage so that it can see different things but still feel relatively safe in its cage. Once you have done this a few times and sense that your parrot is becoming less nervous, you can try to start harness training your parrot. The first few times you take your parrot out in a harness should be relatively short and end on a positive note. A good time to take your parrot out is before it has been fed- this means that when you get back from your walk you can give your bird food and it will associate the walk with a positive end. If your parrot starts to bite you or act agitated, it may be time to end the walk and go back home. Additionally, always make sure to bring some water for your bird if your walk is longer than an hour.

How can I harness train my bird?

The key to successfully training your parrot to wear a harness is time and patience. Every bird is different and requires a different amount of time to accept the harness. However, this process should never be rushed- if it takes months, then so be it. The goal is to have a happy parrot that calmly accepts its harness and is keen to go outside. There are different methods to harness training, but the one we recommend (and which has been tried and tested with Gizmo) is through positive reinforcement.

One of the conditions to starting your harness training is that your parrot should be able to sit on your hand and allow you to touch its body, including its wings.

Step 1: lay the harness near your parrot's cage or play stand, make sure that your parrot can see the harness. This will make sure that your parrot does not see the harness as a scary object when you follow through with the next steps.

Step 2: Let your parrot touch the harness by holding him close to it- do not pressure your parrot. If it is clearly scared, then try the next day. As soon as your bird lets you touch the harness to its beak or body, immediately reward it with his favourite treat. This will help the parrot understand that being near the harness is actually a pleasant experience.

Step 3: If your parrot is now feeling comfortable being near the harness and touching it, the next step is to slip the harness slowly over the neck. It is important to take this step very slowly as it is a scary experience for your bird. Even if you only get the harness halfway around the parrot's neck, still reward it with treats and praise it. Normally after a few tries you should be able to get the harness over its neck completely.

Step 4: The next step and one of the most difficult ones, is to get the harness around the birds' wings. Normally at this stage the parrot should be comfortable with having the harness over its neck, in this case touch your bird lightly under his wings to encourage it to raise them. Reward it with treats as soon as it raises its wing. Repeat several times. Once your parrot easily lifts its wing up, then gently slip the harness around one wing and immediately reward your parrot with treats and praise. Do the same with the second wing if the parrot seems to be relatively calm.

Step 5: The harness should now be fully on your parrot. At first, take your parrot in its harness for a short walk around your house- this will enable him to get used to the harness slowly. Once you have done this a few times, you are ready to go outside for the first time. Keep the sessions short and your parrot should quickly associate the harness with being able to go outside.

Remember that every bird is different and that some will simply never accept a harness, no matter how many treats you give or how many months you try. This can happen and you will simply have to accept this. You should never force a parrot to accept a harness- this will just end with a traumatised parrot which is frightened of you.

A younger parrot which is handfed will accept a harness quite easily compared to an older parrot. However, whilst harness training is generally easier with younger birds, it can also be done with older birds but may take longer and require more patience. Just because an older parrot may take longer to accept a harness, do not give up- sometimes the process can take several months.

Are there any risks to wearing a harness?
-the biggest risks involve a parrot flying off and injuring itself when the harness is only half on, especially if the leash gets caught in a door handle for instance. Other dangers can involve the parrot getting scared and escaping outside if the harness is not held tight.

Please note that unless you are an expert and have managed to teach your parrot recall and free flight, we do not recommend taking your parrot outside without a harness, even if the wings are clipped. No matter how attached your parrot is to you, its first instinct when it gets frightened is to fly away. If your parrot flies away, it can easily starve to death or die from exposure as captive birds cannot take care of themselves on their own. Even parrots with clipped wings can still fly a certain distance, especially if there is a gust of wind. Additionally, smaller parrots can easily become prey to cats, dogs and wild birds such as hawks.

The Eclectus Moult

No matter the species, all parrots moult every year. If you look at your Eclectuses' feathers, you can see that some feathers may look slightly ragged. Damaged feathers can occur through frequent flying, playing and even rubbing against the cage. If damaged feathers never moulted, then they would eventually become useless to the parrot. Moulting enables old feathers to fall out and be replaced by new, healthy feathers so that your Eclectus can continue flying.

Moulting can be a difficult time for your Electus as its feathers will itch when new ones start developing. As its metabolism increases, your parrot may feel more hungry. It is important to feed your parrot additional protein during this time. We have noticed that Gizmo particularly enjoys eating protein-rich foods such as lentils, corn, broccoli and almonds when he is moulting.

New, itchy pin feathers will often make your Eclectus more temperamental and moody. Do not take this personally- this will pass, and your Eclectus may just need to be left alone a bit more during this period. A good way to distract your parrot from his pin feathers is to provide him with new toys or treats. Your parrot may also feel more tired during this time as he is using up a lot of energy to grow new feathers. Earlier bedtimes and a minimum of 12 hours of undisturbed sleep can help give your Eclectus the rest it needs.

Frequent showers are very important during the moulting season- this helps to soothe and moisturise the irritable feathers. Gizmo will let us know that he is irritated if he does not get his daily shower during the moulting season. Aloe Vera sprays can also help to alleviate the itching.

Eclectuses will usually shed their smaller feathers continuously throughout the year, whereas the bigger moults including flight and tail feathers will usually happen in spring and autumn. When you observe your parrot's moults you will quickly notice that moulting happens in a very symmetrical way- a feather which is lost on one wing means that not long after the same feather will be lost on the other wing. This helps Eclectuses fly in a balanced manner.

Moulting is a process that can last several weeks or months. Eclectuses have been observed to generally moult all year round, whereas many other species only moult during spring and autumn. However, Eclectuses have particularly heavy moults during the spring and autumn, even developing bald patches in certain areas. There is a specific moulting pattern which is related to Eclectuses: the Mojo Moult. Not much is known about this moult and not every Eclectus goes through it. The Mojo Moult is named after the first Eclectus (Mojo) who exhibited quite severe balding, especially around the head and neck area. If you notice that your Eclectus is losing more feathers than usual, this may be due to the Mojo Moult which can go on for several months. We do not have much experience with the Mojo moult as Gizmo never went through this phase to date.

If you notice that your parrot is not moulting for quite some time, it may be that the conditions of its environment are delaying the moult. This can happen if there are very little fluctuations in temperature and light. Often, low levels of light can delay the onset of a moult.

Several steps can be taken to encourage a parrot to moult:

-Increase the temperature of the room to around 24-26 degrees Celsius if the room is normally cooler.

-Give your Eclectus frequent showers to encourage preening and softening the feathers in preparation for moulting

-Provide more protein in your parrots' diet, which is needed for new feathers to grow

-Increase the level of light through full spectrum lighting or placing the cage in a sunnier area of the house

-Increase the amount of time your parrot is exposed to light, for example by postponing bedtime by an hour.

Stress lines on feathers

You may notice that certain parrots, especially younger ones, may have black bars across some of their feathers. These are called stress bars and can often happen if a young parrot receives an inadequate diet when the new feathers are just forming, when the temperature is not right (too hot or too cold), or if a parrot has gone through a particularly stressful moment in its life. Often parrots that come from pet stores may have these lines due to a stressful environment. Normally these feathers will moult and be replaced by new, healthy feathers if the parrot's life conditions have positively changed.

Feather Picking, Feather Plucking and Abnormal Moults

Your Eclectuses's feathers should normally look smooth and shiny. Damaged feathers will have a messy look to them: frazzled, bits missing, sticking out or dull-looking. Unfortunately, Eclectuses are particularly prone to feather destruction. The reasons behind this can be endless: boredom, poor nutrition, stress, internal diseases or not enough sleep (amongst others). If a parrot encounters any of these factors in its daily life, then it may resort to feather picking as a means of coping and letting stress out. If you see that your parrot is picking excessively at its feathers or even pulling them out, please make sure to go to a vet to discount any medical issues such as bacteria, parasites, hypovitaminosis or psittacine beak and feather disease (PBFD).

If over-grooming/plucking is not spotted and stopped at the early stages, it can become a habit which is incredibly difficult to break. In this case, the last resort may be to try a collar (with the approval of your veterinary). However, your parrot could easily fall back into its feather picking habits once the collar has been taken off. As such, it is always better to try and find out the root cause for the plucking and try and deal with the original issue itself.

If any medical issues such as viruses and bacteria have been taken out of the equation, then the most common causes of feather plucking are an inadequate diet, stress, lack of exercise or boredom. A severe wing trim or overcrowded cage can also cause a parrot to start plucking. Most of the time, plucking is not linked to only one cause, but rather to several factors. Something as simple as not providing your parrot with enough showers or baths could cause the start of an over-preening behaviour which could then escalate to plucking.

Some of the things which you can try and do to prevent your parrot from over-preening its feather are listed below:

1) Boredom- If your parrot is stuck in its cage all day long on its own, it will definitely be extremely bored and unhappy (wouldn't you be?). Whilst the best option is to have your parrot in its cage as little as possible (ideally only for meal times and for sleep), in practice this is often difficult to do. May of us have full-time jobs which prevent us from spending all day with our parrots. However, there are still many things which you can do to make your parrots' life more interesting while they are in their cage. Firstly, always make sure to have a variety of interesting toys available in the cage such as wooden toys and foraging toys and make sure to rotate the toys and change them frequently. Putting on the radio or the TV when you are gone is also a great way of entertaining your parrot (and teaching it to speak!). Hiding food in difficult to reach places or inside toys is also a great idea to keep your parrot busy throughout the day. Once you get back from work, make sure to spend as much time as possible with your parrot outside of its cage.

2) Light and temperature- Increasing the level of natural sunlight or full-spectrum light could also help over-grooming as it provides a more natural environment for your parrot (In the wild, parrots generally have more sunlight then they are provided when caged). In terms of temperature, make sure that the temperature of your parrot's room is neither too cold nor too warm. Ensure that the room is not too dry either as especially in winter this could be an issue when the heating is on and could irritate the birds' feathers.

3) Make sure that your parrot has the best diet possible with lots of fresh fruit and vegetables and less seeds/pellets or fatty/sugary foods. More details regarding diet for Eclectuses is provided later in the book.

4) If your parrot's wings are clipped and it is not getting the natural exercise it needs by flying, then it could start picking at its feathers out of frustration. A good idea to help your parrot exercise in these circumstances is to teach it to flap its wings. You can do this by taking your parrot on your arm and gently moving your arm up and down- this will cause your parrot to flap its wings in order to balance itself properly.

5) If your parrot is constantly picking at its wings, try and distract it: you can either put on some music, show it a new toy or even just make an unexpected noise. This will distract it from its plucking, at least for a while. However, make sure not to go pick your parrot up as soon as it starts plucking as this could inadvertently be positive reinforcement: If you pluck your wings, I will pick you up and spend some time with you!

Toys

Birds have a natural need to chew wood – in nature this helps them to keep their beaks trimmed and sharp. As such, wooden toys should be made available to all parrots. Whilst wooden toys not only help parrots trim their beaks but also provide great entertainment, special attention should be paid to ensure that wooden toys do not splinter, get wet or excessively dirty. Soft woods and millet woods that do not contain chemicals are preferred to cedar woods as these can contain harmful toxins. Natural is always best, but if you decide to opt for coloured woods, please ensure that these are non-toxic.

In the wild, parrots will use branches, fruit and nuts (amongst others) to play. In captivity, your parrot will often use mostly anything it can reach to investigate and use as a toy, most of which are not safe. By adding a variety of suitable toys to your parrot's cage, you can focus its attention on playing with toys which it can destroy safely.

Vegetable tanned leather toys made specifically for birds can also be provided to your parrot and are usually safe, but you need to make sure that the leather is kept clean in order to prevent growth of bacteria.

Plastic toys are readily available in many stores and are more suited for smaller size parrots as they often include small beads which can be easily broken into pieces by stronger beaks. In general, please make sure to choose toys that are advertised for your parrots' specific size. Toys that are made for cockatiels are not meant for larger parrots like Eclectuses.

Toys made from rope (especially cotton) are often excellent additions to any cage- your parrot will love to climb around and swing on the rope. Often, parrots will also preen the rope strands- this is excellent for feather pluckers who will concentrate on preening the rope rather than their own feathers. However, rope toys should also be monitored as parrots could unfortunately get their legs caught in loose strands and injure themselves. Some parrot owners have found their parrots strangled due to loose strands which managed to get wrapped around the parrots' throat. So please keep a close eye on all of your parrots' toys and remove them if needed.

Toys should be regularly washed in order to prevent bacteria and mould growth. However, make sure not to use any chemicals or softeners which could be harmful to your parrot. A good wash in hot water is generally sufficient to get rid of most dirt and bacteria.

One aspect of bird toys which is often overlooked are the chains which attach the toy to the cage. When choosing toys, pay close attention to the chains- if they are too small and easily detachable then your parrot could swallow it by mistake. A parrot could also get its beak or feet stuck in the chain if it is too small. Some toys use wires as an attachment-these are generally not recommended as wires can easily be bent and injure your parrot.

Make sure that toys which contain various destructible components (for example bells, rings and chains), are too big to fit in your parrot's beak or alternatively are safe to consume.

Toy are often extremely expensive. You do not need to buy toys from pet shops in order to entertain your parrot- simple items such as branches (from trees which are not toxic), nuts with a hard shell and food which is hidden around the cage can make excellent 'toys' for your parrot to entertain himself throughout the day. Other ideas for cheap, interesting toys can be:

-An old t-shirt
-A paper towel
-Toilet paper
-A paper bag
- Wrap a nut or some other treat in many layers of paper- this should occupy your parrot for some time and stimulate its foraging needs.
-Hanging vegetables from a stainless steel skewer in the cage is also an idea to entertain your parrot.

The toys you provide your parrot with should recreate, as much as possible, the type of entertainment it would have in the wild. If your parrot does not have enough enrichment and entertainment, many issues could arise such as over-preening, screaming, stress, boredom and even arthritis from sitting in one spot all day. A good rule is to change your parrot's toys around once a week- this does not mean that you need to provide new toys every week. Simply rotating the toys around in the cage can entertain you parrot and make some toys seem almost 'new' to it. Whilst toys are wonderful additions to cages, make sure that you do not go overboard and overcrowd the cage- a parrot should still have enough space to move around freely and stretch its wings.

If all of this seems a bit complicated, one way you can be certain that your new toy is safe for your parrot is to choose a reputable and well-known toy manufacturer specialised in parrots. Look at buyer reviews and what the company offers. However, even if you buy a toy from a reputable shop, you still need to check the toys regularly to make sure that they are still safe and there is no potential for injury.

Diet

In the wild, Eclectuses will eat native fruits, flowers, nuts and berries. They will often forage for food in the trees unlike many other parrots that pick up food from the ground. Therefore, unlike these parrots (for example African Greys) their diet does not naturally consist of seeds.

All-pellet diets are a very controversial subject in the parrot world. Some vets and parrot owners are big advocates of pellets, stating that pellets are formulated in such a way that all the necessary vitamins and minerals as well as protein/fat ratio have been carefully measured to provide the optimal nutrition for parrots. Others argue that pellets are completely unnatural, and their parrots have developed issues such as toe tapping and feather picking from an all-pellet diet. Additionally, many people argue that all the necessary vitamins and minerals can be provided via a natural diet of fresh fruit, vegetables and grains.

Finally, all-pellet diets are quite simply boring- in the wild parrots eat a large variety of different fruits and vegetables. As such, food should always be presented in an interesting way (foraging for food is a great way of helping parrots exercise their natural instincts). If small quantities of pellets are to be fed, then these should be free of artificial dyes and colours. Our own experience with pellets is not entirely positive- when we first put Gizmo on a pellet diet (with fresh fruits and vegetables), we noticed that he developed toe tapping and wing flipping behaviours. It took us several weeks to figure out the cause for these behaviours. When we removed all pellets from his diet, the wing flipping and toe tapping immediately stopped. Additionally, Gizmo has become so used to a variety of fresh fruit and vegetables every day that he will not touch any pellets at all, even if we provide him with some.

Eclectus parrots require a very specific diet involving a large variety of fresh fruit and vegetables as well as fibre-rich foods due to their digestive tract which is longer than that of most parrots. Because of this long digestive tract, Electuses require a diet low in fat but high in fibre. Eclectuses also require a large quantity of foods rich in Vitamin A. A healthy, balanced diet can prevent many behavioural issues in Eclectuses, specifically feather plucking, screaming and biting.

An Eclectuses' diet should consist of fresh fruit such as mango, papaya, berries and fresh vegetables such as red pepper, carrots and dark, leafy greens. Cooked chick peas, soy beans and lentils are also excellent grains high in fibre. In general, a larger ratio of vegetables to fruits is recommended (for example 70%/30%) as fruits are high in sugars.

Only buy fruits and vegetables that you yourself would be willing to eat- not those that are going off. Organic foods are always best and foods should always be washed properly in order to avoid chemicals and pesticides which could harm your parrot. Although fresh food is always preferable, portions of food can also be frozen and thawed for meals in order to save money and time

Pellets and seeds can also be fed to Eclectuses, but in smaller amounts and should certainly not comprise the bulk of the diet. Nuts should only be given as a treat- these are high in fat and could cause issues such as liver disease and obesity. However, younger Eclectuses require a higher fat diet due to their higher activity levels.

PROTEIN

Eclectuses require protein, especially during certain periods such as when moulting (feathers are partly made of protein), breeding or young Electuses who are growing. A good rule of thumb is 10%-13% protein in your Electuses' diet. Some foods that are high in protein include lentils, chickpeas, almonds, broccoli, and sweet corn.

Finally, remember that it's all about the variety! A good rule to follow is to feed your parrot at the very least five different types of foods every day, especially those that are orange, red or dark green as these contain the important Vitamin A mentioned above.

Below is an example of a healthy daily menu for your Eclectus:

BREAKFAST:

-A mixture of boiled vegetables such as: green beans, carrots and a small portion of broccoli
-A large spoonful of cooked lentils or quinoa
-A portion of boiled sweet potato or pumpkin (Most Eclectuses love both!)
-A small portion of corn on the cob (again, a favourite with Eclectuses)

-Slices of fresh red peppers
-A few blueberries
-Slices of papaya and mango
-A few slices of nuts such as Almonds
- a few boiled chickpeas

The foods should not be too hot or too cold- room temperature is ideal.

THROUGHOUT THE DAY:
-offer a small portion of seeds and nuts (and pellets if you wish) to keep your parrot occupied throughout the day

DINNER:

-Same as for breakfast (variety is key- try different vegetables, fruits and grains to see what your parrot prefers!)

Dangerous foods

The following foods should NEVER be fed to your Eclectus:

-Avocado
-Honey (can cause yeast infections and botulism which compromises the immune system)
-Chocolate
-Foods which are very high in salt and in sugars
-Caffeine
-Certain fruit seeds such as apple seeds
-Legumes which have not been cooked thoroughly (beans such as kidney and lima beans should be cooked for a couple of hours at the very least in order to break down the enzymes which cannot be digested by your parrot).

The list below will provide you with an overview of the sorts of foods you can or cannot feed your Eclectus (and other parrots too!). The list is partly based off our own experiences (as such, you may see items that you consider safe but which we may not) as well as general research.

Safe foods	Foods to be fed in moderation	Unsafe Foods
mango	apple (high sugar)	Avocado
papaya	banana (high sugar)	Rhubarb
red peppers	pears	
pumpkin	oranges (acidic)	The pits and seeds of cherries,
sweet potato	grapes (high sugar)	apples, peaches, apricots, nectarines
carrots	chilli peppers	and plums
Sprouted seeds	corn (high in starch)	
kiwi	brussel sprouts	onions
blueberries	brown rice	cabbage
strawberries		mushrooms
cooked chick peas		alcohol/coffee/coke
cooked lentils		chocolate
cooked fava beans		Walnuts
cooked soy beans		uncooked legumes
dandelion leaves		pasta (starchy)
bok choy		meats
spinach		milk/dairy products
paw paw		iceberg lettuce
Dragonfruit		
zuchinni		
snow peas		
peas		
green beans		
butternut		
brocolli		

WATER:

A good source of clean water is essential for birds, especially those who are fed a diet of dry foods. Water makes up 98% of the molecules in the body. A loss of just 1/10 of a percent of water content may result in death.

Your Eclectus should always have access to fresh, clean water. If you are able to drink your tap water and it is considered safe then usually it is also perfectly safe for parrots. In certain cases it is even preferred to filtered/bottled water as tap water contains minerals such as fluoride which are actually beneficial to our parrot. Finally, make sure to change water every day in order to prevent bacterial growth.

Wing flipping and toe tapping

Wing flipping and toe tapping are two issues which Eclectus owners could encounter:

-Toe tapping is when your parrot's toes open and close involuntarily. This often causes a tapping noise on the branch or rope your parrot is sitting on. Severe toe tapping can prevent a parrot from getting adequate sleep and even cause a parrot to attack its foot out of frustration.

-Wing flipping is when your parrot's wings involuntarily twitch and flap against the body (not once, but continuously). Again, this can prevent your parrot from sleeping and it could attack its wings.

Your parrot could have episodes of toe tapping or wing flipping which after a couple of days stop and never occur again, or alternatively it could be a recurring issue that lasts for months. Whilst it is not known what exactly causes toe tapping and wing flipping, some of the issues which seem to be linked are:

-An inappropriate diet which causes Vitamin A deficiency, calcium deficiency or an imbalance in certain vitamins/minerals. This can be caused by over-feeding a certain type of food or not providing enough variety. Sometimes, too many vitamins (usually through supplemental vitamins) can also cause issues such a toe tapping. Generally, if you feed your Eclectus a balanced diet it should not need any additional vitamins.

-Food allergies (notably to spirulina which is a blue/green algae plant often found in many pellets- some people who have stopped feeding spirulina have noticed a reduction or end to the wing flipping/toe tapping).

-A diet composed entirely of pellets or seeds. In general, Eclectuses who are NOT on a pellet diet seem to have fewer issues such as toe tapping and wing flipping than those who are on a pellet diet. Sometimes, changing pellets to those that are not artificially coloured could also help.

-Stress

How to know if your Eclectus is ill

Parrots are great at hiding illnesses - in the wild, an ill parrot is a vulnerable parrot that could be spotted by a predator and killed. In the wild, even if a parrot is ill, it will try and hide the illness and appear healthy in order to protect itself from predators. As such, parrots often do not show obvious symptoms until the illness has progressed to its later stages. However, as a parrot owner, you should nevertheless be able to spot certain behaviours that could indicate your parrot is sick.

1) If your parrot is sitting low on its perch or at the bottom of the cage- this means that it is probably too weak to hold itself up properly. If you see your parrot doing this, do not hesitate to take your parrot to the vet as soon as possible.

2) If your parrot often has its feathers fluffed/ruffled and sits in a huddled position, this could be an initial indicator that something is wrong, especially if it is doing so whilst standing on two feet. Usually when parrots are cold they will fluff up their wings and also perch on one foot (to keep the other warm- this is not necessarily a sick parrot, but simply slightly cold/tired and ready for bed).

3) Unusual droppings. This is a hard one, as parrot's droppings can often change colour or consistency depending on their diet and what they have just eaten (for example a parrot who has just eaten a handful of blueberries may have very watery droppings. If it has just eaten sweet potato or red peppers, then its droppings could look more orange/red than usual). However, you should frequently examine your parrot's droppings and if you note that the colour is particularly off (yellow or black)/if there is bleeding or a lot of water or undigested food then it may be a good idea to visit the vet.

4) If you notice that your parrot has red, inflamed and runny eyes or nose (called cere), and if there is abnormal discharge then this could also be a sign that something is wrong (for example an infection).

5) If your parrot normally has a good appetite and suddenly stops eating or shows a lack of interest in its favourite foods than this could mean that it has a blockage in his intestine and you should immediately bring your parrot to the vet. The same applies to water- if you

notice your parrot is no longer drinking then it is vital that you bring it to get checked as soon as possible.

6) If your parrot usually likes to preen and keep itself clean (as most healthy parrots should) and you suddenly notice that its feathers are dirty and it has stopped preening them then this could mean that your parrot simply does not have the energy to clean itself and is evidently sick.

These are just some of the symptoms indicating that your parrot could be ill. Always be on the lookout for any changes in your parrot's behaviour - prevention is usually the best cure.

A good way to monitor your parrot' s health is to weigh it weekly. You can buy specific scales for parrots (or even simple gram scales used to weigh food) and weigh it at home. If there is any big change in weight (which for parrots is around 10% of their body weight), then you should bring it to see a vet as weight loss is a common indicator of a sick bird.

Psittacosis

Psittacosis is a severe, bacterial infection which, if left unattended, can lead to your parrot's death. Some early symptoms include nose discharge, green faeces, trouble breathing and a lack of interest in food. The bacterial infection may be treated with antibiotics by your vet.

Psittacine Beak and Feather Disease (PBFD)

This disease, which is caused by a virus, is the only one that is known to directly impact your parrots' feathers causing abnormal, weak feathers and beak growth. Electuses are one of the parrot breeds that are more prone to this disease. You can now test your parrot for this disease through your vet.

What to do if your Eclectus is ill

If your parrot is ill, then you need to follow the steps below in order to provide an optimal environment for your parrot to recover:

-Keep your parrot's cage extremely clean, as a sick bird cannot handle bacteria well due to a weakened immune system.

-Keep you parrot in a warm room (28-32 degrees Celsius). If your notice that your parrot's feet are cold, then increase the temperature accordingly. The temperature should not be too hot (over 35 degrees) nor too cold (under 25 degrees)

-Keep an eye on your parrot and ensure that it is drinking in order to prevent dehydration. Water and food bowls should be kept at a close distance as your parrot may be too weak to climb to the other side of the cage. If you notice your parrot is not eating or drinking, then force-feeding may be necessary and can be discussed with the vet.

-Your parrot should be getting more sleep when it is ill – a minimum of 12 hours is ideal.

-Keep all stands and perches closer to the bottom of the cage, as you parrot is weak and risks falling

-Increase the level of sunlight (without putting the cage directly in the sun) or full-spectrum light as this can decrease stress levels.

Please note that any sign of blood at all is to be taken very seriously and the bleeding should be stopped immediately. If you notice that a pin feather is bleeding, then take your parrot to the vet as soon as possible. In the meantime, you can stop the bleeding by using cornstarch: put some cornstarch on the wound and hold it there for a good 10-20 minutes. Normally this should aid in stopping the bleeding.

Your Eclectuses' cage

You should always provide any parrot with the biggest cage possible for its health and well-being. Eclectuses in particular are large birds with big wing spans and need a cage which is big enough for them to be able to stretch and flap their wings in all safety. Eclectuses love to climb, so providing a tall cage is also a necessity. Stainless steel cages are often the best option as they are easy to clean and widely available. In the cage you should provide a variety of safe toys, perches and ropes for your Eclectus to climb. However, be careful not to overcrowd the cage with toys as this will reduce the space for your Eclectus to stretch its wings and move around.

Ideally your cage should have both a water dish and a water bottle- often Eclectuses will drop pieces of food in their water dish which could quickly lead to bacteria growth. So providing a water bottle can help your parrot have fresh water all day.

The cage should be placed in a room that is not too noisy (for e.g. an office) as Eclectuses do not enjoy a lot of commotion and need to have a place to relax away from all the noise as well as having uninterrupted sleep. Ideally, the room should have a window as this will provide natural daylight for your parrot and provide a source of entertainment. However, the cage should not be placed where it will get direct sunlight as your parrot could easily overheat. If you live in a cold climate, then you need to make sure that the room can be easily heated in winter (and cooled down in summer).

If you can place the cage so that one side of the cage is close to a wall then that is ideal as it feels more 'safe' for your parrot that can retreat to the corner if he wants to.

The lining of your cage can be a variety of materials (if your cage has a metal grid at the bottom this is recommended for hygiene purposes). Some of the popular materials which bird owners use are wood shavings and newspaper.

When choosing a cage, you should also make sure that the spacing of the cage bars is adequate for your species of parrot. Your parrot should not be able to stick its head between the cage bars, but the cage bars should also not be spaced so close together that your parrot could get its toes stuck when climbing.

A lot of people like to cover their parrot's cage at night as this will often calm and quieten the parrot for bedtime. However, this is not a necessity if your parrot' cage is in a sufficiently dark room for the night. If you do decide to cover the cage, then you should stick to doing so every evening as parrots are creatures of habit and covering one night but not the other could cause them unnecessary stress.

Aside from a cage, you should also invest in a playstand for your parrot, which unlike the cage will be situated in a busy area of the house such as the living room where your parrot can join you when you are home. Play stands come in all shapes and sizes - from large java trees to smaller table stands. Bigger is often better and the play stand should also include a variety of toys for your parrot to entertain itself as well as a couple of cups for food and water. Java trees make great play stands- we have one set up for Gizmo in our living room and he tends to spend most of his time on it.

You should clean your bird's cage frequently in order to prevent bacteria growth and illnesses caused by a dirty environment. Make sure to change the paper at the bottom of the cage everyday (especially if you feed your parrot fresh fruit and vegetables) in order to prevent the growth of fungus. Food and water cups should also be cleaned every day. The cage grate should be washed every week (as should the cage ideally). Perches and toys can be left for longer periods of time between washes (unless they are particularly dirty). Make sure to use safe products when cleaning your parrot's cage. You can either find specific parrot cleaning products at certain stores or you can use baking powder as a scrub (and make sure to rinse the cage well).

Showering your Eclectus

Many parrots love to bathe, but none more so than the Eclectus parrot. Gizmo is a particular fan of showers and will jump up and down with excitement when we mention the word "shower". Bathing your parrot regularly should be part of your weekly routine. Water not only cleans your parrot's feathers but also encourages it to preen and removes any pollutants from its feathers. Bathing can also help moisturise feathers and subsequently prevent plucking in some cases. You can bathe your parrot in several ways:

-By providing a perch in the shower and placing a gentle stream of water on your parrot (make sure that your parrot has enough space to move out of the water if it wants to do so)
-Holding your parrot directly under a shower head set on a low intensity (again, make sure

that your parrot can move its head out of the way of the water stream as some parrots hate getting their head wet)

-Many parrots love the sound of running water and will stick their heads under the sink faucet if you let them!

-Providing a big bowl of water in your parrot's cage (this is easier for smaller sized birds such as budgies)

-If your parrot is comfortable enough, you can also spray it with warm water (some parrots love to be misted with water and others are frightened of spray bottles-do not force your parrot to do something it does not want to do). Gizmo for example hates sprays of any kind and will run away from them.

When bathing your parrot, make sure that the temperature of the water is not too hot and not too cold (room temperature is a good compromise). Bathing should also be done in the mornings or during the day but your parrot should never go to bed still wet as it can easily get ill.

Some people like to blow-dry their parrot. We do not recommend this as firstly, it is not natural and can over dry the skin, causing itchiness. Secondly, some blow-dryers have non-stick properties which can be dangerous for your bird.

Whilst you find a variety of different bathing products in your pet shop, warm water is enough to properly bathe your parrot. In some cases, Aloe Vera products aimed for parrots can help itchy or dry skin and can be added in small quantities to your water bottle spray.

Eclectuses have very particular feathers as they use their oil glands for lubrication – this means that their feathers are particularly oily compared to other breeds and often you will notice that water just glides over the feathers without actually penetrating- this is perfectly normal and does not mean that your parrot is waterproof. It just means that you may need to shower your parrot for a little longer until the feathers have absorbed the water well. Misting Eclectuses with water sprays can also help the water to clean the feathers well.

Bathing is particularly important if your parrot is a plucker or during the moulting season as you parrot will feel particularly itchy and uncomfortable.

Wing Clipping

Another controversial subject in the parrot world is wing clipping.
Although leaving a bird flighted is more natural, healthy and humane, wing clipping may sometimes be necessary in certain households.

Firstly let's talk about the advantages of flight:

-Flying is the best form of exercise your parrot can get and can prevent obesity and strokes
-Flying can increase your bird's confidence and prevent issues such as depression and feather plucking
-In case of danger, your parrot can easily get out of the way
-Flying is the most natural thing for a bird- it is what they do most of the day in the wild

As explained previously, in certain circumstances it may be a good idea to clip your parrot's wings. Amongst others:

-If you have young children who could leave a window or door open, in which case a flighted bird could escape or fly out by accident. Unfortunately this happens more often than people think.
-Clipping your parrot's wings when you first get it can help you to train and tame your parrot
-When being introduced to your house for the first time, clipping your parrot's wings can prevent it from getting spooked and flying off into walls or windows and injuring itself

Some of the side effects of wing clipping can be the following:

-A parrot whose wings have been badly clipped could fall heavily to the floor if it tries to fly, which could cause serious injuries.
-Wing clipping can sometimes result in parrots that are frightened more easily and less sure of themselves

Wing clipping methods:

There are several methods to clipping wings. Below are some of the advantages and disadvantages of each:

-Clipping the outer primaries: this is the most common and allows your parrot to safely fly a short distance.
-Clipping only one wing: this is not recommended as it will cause balance issues for your parrot and could cause it to drop to the floor and injure itself if it tries to fly.

-Plucking the feathers: unfortunately this is also a method that some people use but we consider it inhumane and extremely uncomfortable for your parrot- the feathers will also grow back within a couple of months.

Do not forget that clipping a parrot's wings is not irreversible- the clipped feathers will go through the moulting process like any other feather and new ones will grow in their place (the time can vary but usually clipped feathers should be completely replaced within the space of a year. However, a parrot whose wings are clipped at a young age when it is just learning to fly may never learn to fly as well as it should, even when the feathers have grown back. Your parrot may also feel less confident with flying and it may take you some time to train your parrot to fly and rebuild its flight muscles.

Clipping your parrot's wings does not mean that it is safe to take your parrot outside- a clipped parrot can still fly a short distance and if something scares your bird whilst it is outside, it can certainly fly off (to most people's surprise and regret). Even if your parrot does not get frightened, all it takes is a strong gust of wind to blow your parrot away.

Whilst you can clip your parrot's feather yourself, unless you are completely sure of the process, it is always recommended to go to a vet or a specialist. If you accidentally cut a blood feather then you could not only cause great pain to your parrot, but also bleeding of the feather which is difficult to stop.

Nail Clipping

In the wild, parrots' nails are worn down naturally as they climb around and hang from trees and branches. However, this is often not the case in captivity and therefore we need to trim the nails occasionally so that they do not get too long and it becomes uncomfortable for the parrot to perch. Nail clipping is very important and should be done as soon as your bird's nails get too sharp and holding your parrot becomes painful. If you let your bird's nails get too long then perching will become uncomfortable and your parrot's nails could get caught in toys or its cage, leading to potential injuries.

Trimming nails can be done at home and does not require a visit to the vet (unless your parrot is extremely difficult to handle or if you feel more comfortable having a professional trim the nails). The prerequisite is that your parrot should be comfortable with being held and handled on a daily basis. When trimming nails, you should be careful not to trim too far back or your parrot's nail could start bleeding and the experience could be very uncomfortable and painful for your bird. Normally just trimming the very tips of the nails should be sufficient. Nails that are too short can also cause issues for your parrot who will not be able to grip onto surfaces properly.

One way to help your parrot keep his nails trimmed naturally is to provide a sand perch or grooming perch specifically designed to wear down your parrot's nails and beak (this can be found in most parrot shops).

When trimming your parrot's nails, you can use simple nail clippers (although for bigger parrots you may require bigger clippers such as those designed for dogs). You should always have cornstarch at hand in case you trim the nail too far and it starts bleeding. The cornstarch will help to stop the bleeding in this case. You can begin by wrapping your parrot gently in a towel to keep it still and prevent it from flying off (a second person is useful in this case as they can hold the parrot while you trim the nails). Be careful not to hold your parrot too tightly as you could suffocate it if too much pressure is put on its chest. Remember to only cut the very tips and try and trim the nails as quickly as possible not too tire or stress your parrot out for too long. If your parrot is visibly in distress, then end the nail trimming session immediately and reward your parrot so that it associates the experience with something positive.

Another method (which is less stressful and more natural), is to play with your parrot with the nail clippers so that it gets used to them over time and once it accepts them you can try and incorporate nail trimming while your parrot is out and about playing or distracted by something, or even just relaxing on a perch. Just be careful that your parrot does not move too much when you actually trim the nails. Some parrots like cockatoos who love to be handled will even enjoy the nails trimming session as they will feel pampered and taken care of. These last two methods of course require trust and a good bond with your parrot.

Occasionally there are situations when you should not trim your parrot's nails- often older birds are clumsy and if your trim their nails too much then they will find it very difficult to perch properly. The same applies to sick or weak parrots. Trimming young parrot's nails is also not recommended as they are learning to balance themselves and grip onto different surfaces.

Top 8 Household Dangers to Pet Birds

As parrot owners we need to be aware of the many household dangers our birds could encounter and try and make the house as safe a place as possible. This is particularly the case because of the small size of parrots, their sensitive respiratory system and their ability to fly. Additionally, parrots are curious creatures by habit and often find a way of getting themselves into trouble.

1. Poisoning: Birds have a very sensitive respiratory system and therefore can easily get ill or even die if they inhale certain toxins that are frequently found in the average household. Amongst others, here is a list of dangerous substances which should not be used in a parrot home:

-Insecticides
-Cigarette smoke
-Candles
-Ammonia
-Perfume and incense- whilst not necessarily deadly, both of these can irritate your parrot's nostrils and cause discharge or redness
-Bleach
-Nail polish remover
-Paint and glue

2. Diet: Unfortunately, a bad or unhealthy diet can often be the biggest danger for our parrots. Whilst certain foods such as avocado and chocolate are toxic for your parrot, an all-seed diet can also cause health and behavioural issues, even leading to shorter lifespans for our birds.

3. Wires and cables: Birds are curious by nature and exposed wires and cables can be dangerous if your parrot decides to bite into them. Always make sure to keep these away from your bird and always monitor your parrot when it is out.

4. Toys: As explained previously, many toys can be considered unsafe for your parrot, especially those that have small parts that can be easily swallowed or rope toys with frayed ends which could strangle your parrot if it gets caught in them.

5. Windows and mirrors: Your parrot could easily get confused by a mirror or a window and mistakenly fly into them causing serious damage and even death in some cases if your bid hits them at full speed. Make sure to monitor your parrot when it is out around windows and mirrors and covering them could also be a solution. When you first bring your parrot into your home, make sure to walk around with it and let it touch all the windows and mirrors in your house so that it gets used to them and realises that they are hard. Leaving windows open around a flighted bird is also a danger as it could escape and unfortunately a mistake that many people have done and live to regret.

6. Pets: Whilst parrots can get along with other pets in your home, the prey instinct is always there in dogs and cats who could easily get excited by a bird in flight and bite it by accident. Always keep a close watch when all of your pets are out together and don't forget that dog and cat saliva (not to mention human saliva) can be dangerous for your parrot. Many people think it is fun or cute to give their parrot a wet kiss on the beak or to let them explore your mouth, but human saliva can make a parrot very ill if ingested enough.

7. **Trees and plants**: Some trees and plants can be dangerous for your parrot, especially Christmas trees and plants that have had chemicals added to them.

8. **Non-stick coatings:** Items such as pans and irons which have non-stick coatings (such as Teflon products)- the fumes from these items if overheated are extremely dangerous for your parrot. Alternatives for Teflon pots and pans are ceramic ones- these are great and non-toxic.

Epilogue

We hope that this short book has given you a better insight into the world of Eclectus ownership and parrots in general. Please remember that every parrot is an individual and not everything that has been written here is applicable to all parrots, but should simply be taken as a guideline.

Owning an Eclectus is a big responsibility, but one that brings with it a lot of joy, laughter and love. Although you need to be ready for some of the difficuties that go along with owning a parrot (cleaning, cooking and more cleaning), these should not discourage you from the decision to get an Eclectus parrot. Like any pet, there will be days when you get frustrated and tired. However, it is all worth it when your Eclectus gives you a kiss or cuddles up to you. At the end of the day, what other pet can say 'I love you'? If taken good care of, your Eclectus can live a very long time and keep you company for the rest of your life.

In our personal opinion (albeit slightly biased), there is no better companion than an Eclectus. From their ability to bond strongly with their owners to their amazing speaking abilities, there is nothing that these beautiful parrots cannot do.

Made in the USA
Coppell, TX
16 June 2021

57503262R00043